Jesus, Friend of Children

**The life of Jesus
told in forty
stories for young
readers**

SANDY
LANE
BOOKS

Mary's Strange Visitor

One day, many hundreds of years ago, in a little town called Nazareth, Mary had a visitor.

Mary was engaged to be married. Joseph, who was to be her husband, was the village carpenter.

Mary and Joseph, like all the people of the country of Israel at that time, longed for the day when God would help their country again. He had promised to send them a King who would set them free. But everything seemed hopeless. Their enemies, the Romans, occupied their country. All the news was bad news.

Then one day, as Mary was busy with her work, she had a very surprising visitor. It was an angel, a messenger from God himself.

'Don't be afraid,' the angel said. 'I have come with good news. God loves you and has specially chosen you to be the mother of the promised King. You will have a baby boy. And you are to call him Jesus. He will be very great – the Son of God himself.'

Mary was longing to ask questions. There was so much she did not understand. But she simply said, 'I am willing to do whatever God wants.'

LUKE I :26–38

Mary Goes on a Visit

A few days later, Mary set out to visit her cousin, Elizabeth. For many years Elizabeth and her husband Zechariah had prayed for a son. Now at last God had answered their prayers. Elizabeth, too, was expecting a baby.

When Mary arrived at her cousin's house, Elizabeth's heart sang for joy as she welcomed her in. She knew at once the wonderful news Mary had come to bring.

Mary's heart, too, overflowed with happiness.

'I cannot help singing God's praise,' she said. 'He has made me glad. I am nothing, yet God my Saviour has done such wonderful things for me. And his love and goodness goes out to all mankind.'

Mary stayed with Elizabeth for about three months. Then she went back home to Nazareth.

LUKE 1:39–56

The Baby Born in a Stable

The Roman Emperor gave his orders. He wanted
a list of all his people, to make sure they paid their
taxes. Like everyone else, Joseph had to register at
the town his ancestors came from. So Mary and
Joseph began the long journey to Bethlehem.

It was late when they arrived, and Mary was
very tired. And then the inn was already full! The
only shelter they could find was in the stable with
the animals.

That night Mary's baby was born.

She wrapped him warmly in the clothes she had
brought, and laid him to sleep in the manger which
held food for the animals.

Out on the dark hills shepherds were guarding
their flocks. Suddenly the sky was a blaze of light.
The men shook with fear. Then an angel spoke to
them:

'Don't be afraid,' he said. 'I have come with
wonderful news. The Saviour has come – born this
very night in Bethlehem.'

Then the sky was full of angels, all singing God's
praise.

'Glory to God in highest heaven,' they sang.
'And peace to men on earth.'

When the angels had gone and the sky was dark
again, the shepherds looked at one another.

'Let's go to Bethlehem,' they said, 'and see what
has happened.'

So they came to the town and found Mary and
Joseph in the stable of the inn. And when they saw
the baby lying in the manger they knew that all the
angels had said was true.

LUKE 2:1–20

6

Strangers From the East

Some weeks later, three strangers from the east –
wise men who studied the stars – arrived at the
king's palace in Jerusalem.

'Where can we find the baby who is born to be
King of the Jews?' they asked. 'We saw his star rise
and have come to worship him.'

The king consulted his advisers. 'When the

promised King comes he will be born in Bethlehem,'
they said. So the strangers travelled on, still following
the star that had led them all the way. They found
the baby in Bethlehem with Mary his mother. And
they fell on their knees and worshipped him. Out of
their bags they brought presents – strange, rich
presents to give to a baby! – gold and frankincense
and myrrh.

MATTHEW 2

The Day Jesus was Lost

Jesus was twelve. Every year, in the Spring, Joseph and Mary went to Jerusalem for the Passover Festival. This time Jesus went with them. Happy groups of visitors crowded into the city from all over Israel.

The busy, exciting days of the Festival were soon over and it was time to go home. Mary and Joseph set off with a crowd of friends and neighbours returning to Nazareth. They thought Jesus was with the other boys, and walked all day before they noticed he was missing. No one had seen him. Mary and Joseph were too worried to sleep that night. At dawn they were up and on their way back to Jerusalem to look for him.

Another whole day went by before they found him. Jesus was in the Temple, God's house, listening to the teachers of the Jewish Bible and asking questions. Everyone who heard him was amazed at how much he understood.

'Why did you do this to us?' Mary asked. 'Your father and I have been so worried.'

Jesus seemed almost surprised at her question. 'But surely you knew I had to be here in my Father's house?' he said.

The family returned to Nazareth, and Jesus was the loving, obedient son he had always been. He grew tall and strong. He was clever and thoughtful. God loved him, and so did all who knew him.

LUKE 2:41–52

The King's Messenger

Elizabeth's son, John, was born three months before Jesus. God made it plain that he had chosen John for a special purpose. It was John's task to prepare God's people for the coming of the promised King.

John's father, Zechariah, helped his young son to learn and understand the scriptures – the Law of God and the words of the prophets. John was being trained for the work that lay ahead. It was a hard life.

When he grew older he lived alone in the desert, wearing a rough camel-skin coat and leather belt, and eating locusts and the honey of wild bees. There, in the desert, God gave John his message. He began to preach and teach – and crowds flocked to hear this strange, wild-looking man who spoke with such power.

'God's King is coming soon,' John said. 'Make sure you are ready for him. Turn away from your sins. From now on you must live to please God.'

Many of those who heard him did turn from their old ways – and John baptized them in the River Jordan. It was as if they were being washed clean in the river.

One day Jesus came from Nazareth to be baptized by John. As soon as he saw Jesus, John knew that this was God's promised King.

'I really ought to be baptized by you,' he said. 'Yet you come to me.'

But he did as Jesus asked and baptized him. As Jesus came up out of the water, he heard a voice from heaven saying:

'This is my own dear Son. He rejoices my heart.'

MATTHEW 3:1–17; MARK 1:1–11; LUKE 3:1–22

The Four Fishermen

After his baptism Jesus stayed in the desert for forty days. All that time he had nothing to eat, and was tempted to disobey God. But he stayed firm and did not give in.

Jesus went back home, but from now on his life was different. He no longer worked in the carpenter's shop at Nazareth. Instead, he went to a town by the Lake of Galilee and began to tell people the Good News from God. It was a message about a new kind of life. And he began to cure people of all kinds of illness. He made the blind see and cripples walk. He made sick minds and bodies whole again.

Lake Galilee was a good place for fishing. Many of the local people earned their living as fishermen. Jesus was walking by the lake one day when he saw two brothers – Simon Peter and Andrew – out fishing in their boat.

'Come with me,' he called to them. 'And I will teach you to catch, not fish, but people!'

They came ashore at once and went with him. A little further along, James and John were mending their nets. Jesus called them too, and they left their nets and went with him.

MATTHEW 4:12–22; MARK 1:14–20

A Roman Soldier Believes in Jesus

Soon Jesus was busy from morning till night. He never had a moment to himself. Wherever he went, crowds gathered. He was full of love and pity for the poor and helpless, the children, and all who suffered. He was often tired. But no one who needed him was ever turned away.

One day an officer from the enemy troops occupying the country came to Jesus and asked his help.

'My servant is very ill,' he said, '– so ill, I am afraid he may die.'

'I will come at once and make him better,' Jesus said.

'I am not worthy to have you in my home,' the officer answered. 'You have only to say the word and my servant will be well again. I know, because I too give orders. I tell my soldiers what to do and they do as I say.'

Jesus was astonished that the man had such trust in him. He turned to the people who were with him and said:

'I have not found faith like this man's in the whole land of Israel.'

Then he said to the officer: 'Go home now. What you have believed has already happened.'

And from that moment the servant was well again.

MATTHEW 8:5–13

The Widow's Son who Lived Again

Soon after this, Jesus went to a town called Nain. As he reached the town gate, a funeral procession was coming out. A poor widow's only son had died, and a great crowd of friends and neighbours was with her. Jesus was full of pity for the woman.

'Stop crying!' he said to her, kindly.

Then he went over to the stretcher, and the men who were carrying it stopped.

'Young man,' Jesus commanded. 'Get up!'

At once the dead man sat up and began to talk – and Jesus gave him back to his mother.

Jesus went from village to village. He preached to all kinds of people and healed all sorts of illnesses. He told the people they could know God as their Father, and that he would give them a new life.

The four fishermen from Galilee went with him, and so did other friends. There were women, too, who went to look after them all – and to listen to Jesus. Ordinary people flocked to hear him. When Jesus looked at the crowds he was filled with pity for them. They were tired and lost – like sheep without a shepherd.

LUKE 7:11–17

The Woman at Simon's House

A rich man called Simon invited Jesus home for dinner. As they were sitting down to eat, a woman came in, carrying a jar of expensive sweet-scented oil. She was known to be a bad woman. Decent people, like Simon, would have nothing to do with her. But she had heard that Jesus was there, and she was determined to see him.

As she knelt at Jesus' feet, the tears came. She kissed his feet and dried them with her long hair. Then she broke the seal on the jar and poured out the oil. Its fragrance filled the room.

'How can Jesus bear to let this woman near him?' Simon thought. 'Everyone knows what she is like.'

Jesus knew what Simon was thinking.

'There were once two men who borrowed money from a money-lender,' he said to Simon. 'One borrowed a lot, the other only a little. Neither could pay the money back, so the money-lender forgave both and let them off. Which do you think loved him more after that?'

'The one who was forgiven more,' Simon said.

'That's right,' Jesus said. 'Now, look at this woman. You provided no water for me to wash my dusty feet when I came in: she has washed them with her tears. You gave me no kiss of welcome: she has kissed my feet. You did not pour oil on my head: she has poured it on my feet. It's true that she has lived a bad life but her love shows that her sins are forgiven.'

And Jesus said to the woman:

'Your sins are forgiven. Your faith has saved you. Go in peace.'

LUKE 7:36–50

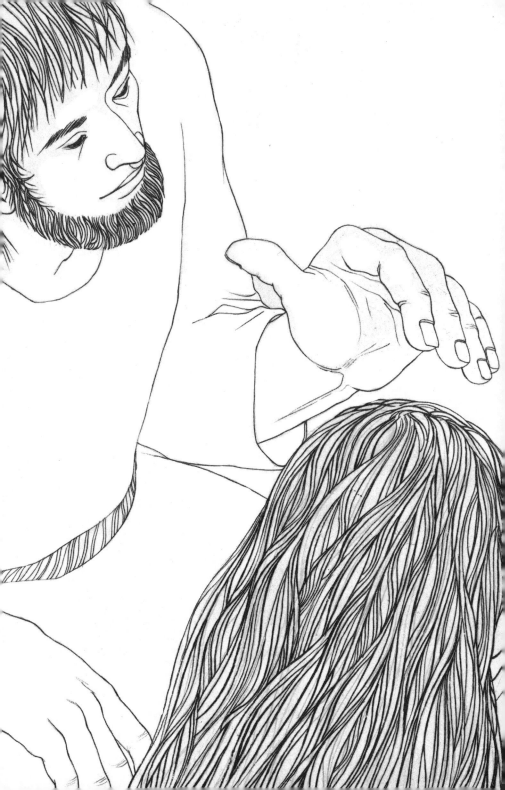

Twelve Special Friends

One evening Jesus went up into the hills and spent all night praying to God. Next morning he chose twelve of his followers to be his special friends (the twelve apostles).

They were the four fishermen – Simon Peter and Andrew, James and John; Philip and Bartholomew; Matthew (who had been a cheating tax collector) and Thomas the twin; another James and Simon the patriot; Judas and another man with the same name – Judas Iscariot, the one who in the end turned traitor.

These twelve men went everywhere with Jesus. They were his friends and he was their Teacher. He sent them out to tell people the Good News and to heal the sick. They shared his life, leaving home and family to go with him.

Like Jesus, they were often tired and hungry. Sometimes there was nowhere for them to rest or sleep. But it was worth it to be Jesus' friends. They saw the wonderful things he did. And he explained to them what God had sent him to do.

MARK 3:13–19; LUKE 6:12–16

The Secret of a Happy Life

When Jesus was out on the hillside one day a great crowd came to hear him. He made them sit down and began to teach.

'You think it's the rich who are happy', he said, 'because they have all they want. But you are wrong.'

He turned to his followers and said:

'Happy are you poor: the kingdom of God is yours!

Happy are you who are hungry now: you will be filled!

Happy are you who weep now: God will comfort you!

Happy are you when men hate and reject you for being my friends.

Great is your reward in heaven!'

Jesus saw that the people were puzzled. So he went on:

'Don't try to get rich here on earth, where burglars can break in and steal your treasures. Store up riches in heaven where no one can rob you.

'You worry too much about food and clothes. If God can look after the birds, and dress the flowers so beautifully, won't he look after you, too? You matter much more to him than they do. Put God and what he says first, and he will give you all you need.'

Jesus used word-pictures to help people understand. 'You are like salt,' he said. 'Salt adds flavour and stops food going bad. You must be like that in the world. Your lives must shine like lights. Then everyone will see the good you do, and thank God for it.'

MATTHEW 5:1–16; 6:19–34

High Standards

Jesus talked about God's rules for life, the 'Ten Commandments'. He said we must not even think bad things, let alone do them.

Of course, we do not kill anyone; but do we have nasty, hateful thoughts about them, which is just as bad?

God wants us to love everyone, enemies as well as friends. When someone is unkind, we must be kind – not unkind – back. When someone is spiteful, we must be loving.

'Give more than people ask,' Jesus said. 'And when you help someone in need, keep it secret. Don't show off about it.'

Peter asked: 'How often must I go on forgiving someone who wrongs me? Twenty times?' Jesus answered, 'No, that's not enough. You must go on and on forgiving, every single time.'

MATTHEW 5; 18:21–22

How to Pray

'When you pray,' Jesus said, 'don't make a great fuss about it. Go into your room, shut the door, and pray to God your Father. There's no need to use long words, or to go on and on. He knows all your needs. So pray simply, like this:

"Our Father in heaven:
May your name be kept holy,
May your kingdom come,
May your will be done on earth as it is in heaven.
Give us today the food we need;
Forgive us the wrongs that we have done,
As we forgive those who have wronged us.
Do not bring us into temptation,
But deliver us from the Evil One."

'Ask, and you will receive,' Jesus said. 'Seek, and you will find. Knock, and the door will be opened.'

MATTHEW 6:5–15; 7:7–8

Jesus Tells Some Stories

When Jesus spoke, everyone listened. Even the children were quiet, hoping for a story. Jesus used stories (parables) to explain things that were hard to understand. He wanted people to think about them, find their special meaning, and learn about God. 'If you have ears,' he often said, 'then listen.' He meant, 'Think hard, and try to understand.'

'There was a man who took a tiny mustard seed,' Jesus said. 'And he planted it in his field. It was so small it was like a speck of dust. But the little seed grew. Soon it was a strong plant. It grew and grew till it was like a great tree and birds built nests in its branches.

'God's new kingdom is like that. It grows and grows as more and more people are added to it.'

MATTHEW 13:31-32

The Lost Sheep

On the hills little flocks of sheep were grazing –
each flock cared for by the shepherd. One day Jesus
told this story.

'A shepherd had 100 sheep. One of the sheep got
lost in the hills. So the shepherd left all the others
safe in the fold and searched for the lost sheep. He
was so happy when at last he found it. He picked
the sheep up and carried it home on his shoulders.
Then he called all his friends and neighbours.

'Come and celebrate with me,' he said. 'I have
found the sheep that was lost.'

'There is joy like that in heaven,' Jesus said,
'over everyone who returns to God. I have come to
search for those who have strayed from God's paths,
and bring them back.'

LUKE 15:1–7

The Good Neighbour

'Teacher,' Jesus was once asked, 'what must I do to receive this life you are telling us about?'

'What does the Bible say?' Jesus answered.

'Love God with all your heart and soul and mind and strength,' the man replied, 'and your neighbour as yourself.'

'That's right,' Jesus said.

'But who is my neighbour?' the man asked.

So Jesus told him this story.

'A man was going down the lonely road from Jerusalem to Jericho, when robbers sprang out from behind the rocks. They beat him up, took his money, and left him.

'After a little while a priest came by. He saw the man lying there, but did nothing to help.

'Then a Jewish teacher came along. He went over and looked at the man, but he did not help.

'A foreigner, a Samaritan, came next. He stopped and cleaned the man's wounds with wine and soothing oil. Then he bandaged him, put him on his own donkey, and took him to an inn.

'Next day he had to leave, but he gave the inn-keeper some money. "Take good care of him," he said. "And if it costs more, I'll pay you when I come back." He did all this for a total stranger, not even one of his own people.'

Jesus turned to the man who had asked the question. 'Now which of these was a true neighbour to the man who was hurt?'

'The one who was kind to him.'

'Then go, and do as he did.'

LUKE 10:25–37

34

The King on his Throne

'One day you will see me come as King,' Jesus once said. 'I shall sit on my throne and all the nations of the world will be gathered before me. Then I will separate the people just as a shepherd separates sheep from goats – one group on my right, the other on my left.

'Then I will say to those on my right: "My Father loves you. Come and live in God's kingdom, in the place made ready for you from the very beginning. For I was hungry and you gave me food. I was thirsty and you gave me drink. I was a stranger and you took me into your home. I had nothing to wear and you clothed me. I was ill and in prison and you came to see me."

' "But when did we do those things for you?" the people will ask. And I will answer: "Whenever you were kind and loving to other people you were kind and loving to me."

'Then I will turn to those on my left and say: "Go away; I never want to see you again. For I was hungry and you did not give me food. I was thirsty and you gave me nothing to drink. I was cold, a stranger, sick and in prison – and you never lifted a finger to help."

' "But when did we refuse you help?" they will ask. And I will answer: "Whenever you refused help to other people you refused help to me."

'And they will be sent away and punished. But the others will enjoy fullness of life.'

MATTHEW 25:31–46

Two Men in God's Temple

There are some people who think they are better than everyone else. They are proud and look down on other people. Jesus told a story about someone like that.

'Two men went to the Temple to pray,' Jesus said. 'One was a strict, religious man whom everyone looked up to. The other was a cheating tax collector.

'The religious man was proud and full of himself. He prayed like this: "I do thank you, God, that I am better than other people. I go without food twice a week and give away a lot of my money. I am not a cheat, like that tax collector over there."

'But the tax collector stood with bowed head, just inside the door. He hardly dared speak to God, he was so ashamed of himself. "Oh God," he confessed, "I have done so many wrong things. Please forgive me – though I know I don't deserve it." '

And Jesus said: 'I tell you, it was the tax collector, not the man who was proud, who went home forgiven. For God loves a humble man who is willing to admit his faults.'

LUKE 18:9–14

Blind Bartimaeus

Bartimaeus was blind. He could not work for his living. Instead he sat beside the dusty road, day in, day out, begging for food and money from passers-by. He longed to be like other people – to be able to see and go to work and enjoy life. He had heard stories of how Jesus cured all kinds of illness. And he had made up his mind that if ever Jesus came to his town, he would ask his help.

Then one day Bartimaeus heard the noise of a great crowd coming along the road.

'What is it?' he asked. 'Tell me what you can see.'

'It's Jesus – he's coming this way,' they told him.

Bartimaeus could not see, but there was nothing wrong with his voice! And he wasn't going to let Jesus go by without noticing him. So he began to shout: 'Jesus of Nazareth! Jesus, have mercy on me!' He made so much noise that people got annoyed with him. But he would not stop shouting.

Then Jesus stopped and called Bartimaeus to him. Bartimaeus was so eager to get there, he threw down his cloak and came running.

'What do you want me to do?' Jesus asked.

'I want to see again,' Bartimaeus answered.

'Your faith has made you well,' Jesus said.

At once Bartimaeus was able to see. And he joined the crowd that was following Jesus.

MARK 10:46–52

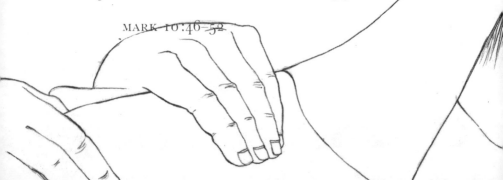

On the Mountain Top

The twelve disciples had been with Jesus a long time now. The better they knew him, the more they loved him. At first they did not really understand who he was. Now they began to realise that he was God's promised King.

But Jesus had many enemies as well as friends. He knew that there was trouble ahead, and spoke to the twelve about it.

Three of his friends – Peter, James and John – were specially close to him. One day Jesus took them to the top of a high and lonely hill.

As he prayed, they saw a change come over him. His face shone bright as the sun, and his clothes as white as light. A shining cloud came over them, and a voice from the cloud said:

'This is my own dear Son – listen to him.'

The three friends were so frightened that they threw themselves down on the ground, hiding their faces. But Jesus came and touched them.

'Get up,' he said. 'Don't be afraid.'

And when they looked up, there was Jesus, just as usual. The cloud and the dazzling light had gone.

As they came down the hill, Jesus said to them:

'Don't tell anyone about this. Keep it secret until I am raised from death.'

MATTHEW 17:1–9

Getting and Giving

Two brothers were quarrelling about their father's will. Jesus said to the people:

'Don't be greedy, always wanting more. Real life isn't just a matter of getting rich.' Then he told them a story.

'There was a farmer who was very rich. His land was good. It grew fine crops. His barns weren't big enough to store them all.

So he thought to himself, "I'll pull down the old barns and build bigger ones. Then I'll have room for all my crops. There'll be enough to last me for years. I'll be able to take things easy and enjoy myself. No more work for me."

'But God said to him: "You stupid man. This very night you die. Then who will get all this?" '

Then Jesus said to the people, 'If you spend your life piling up money and possessions, never giving a thought to God, you are just as stupid as that farmer. Love God, do all you can to please him – and he will look after you.'

Some time later, Jesus stood in the Temple, watching the rich toss their coins into the offering-box. Then a poor widow came by and dropped in two very small coins. Jesus turned to the disciples and said:

'This poor widow has really given more than all the rest put together. They only gave what they had to spare – but she has given her last penny.'

LUKE 12:13–31; 21:1–4

45

Jesus, Friend of Children

One day people brought their little children to
Jesus and asked him to bless them. But the
disciples scolded them and tried to turn them away.

'Don't bother Jesus now,' they said. 'Can't you
see he's busy?'

But Jesus called the children to him.

'Let them come to me,' he said. 'Don't stop
them. For the kingdom of God belongs to people
like this. Only those who come to God like little
children will enter his kingdom.'

Then he took them in his arms and prayed that
God would bless them.

MARK 10:13–16

Food for Five Thousand!

Jesus went into the hills with his disciples, and a great crowd followed. When evening came, everyone was hungry. They were a long way from the nearest village.

'Send them away to buy food,' the disciples said.

'No,' said Jesus, 'we must give them something to eat before they go.'

'But we haven't enough money to buy food for all these people,' the disciples answered.

Then Andrew, Peter's brother, said:

'There's a boy here who has five barley loaves and two small fish. But they won't go far amongst all these people!'

'Tell everyone to sit down on the grass,' Jesus said. There was a crowd of about five thousand people.

Jesus took the boy's bread and fish and gave thanks to God. The disciples took the food round – and to their great surprise everyone had more than enough to eat. Even the left-overs filled twelve baskets!

JOHN 6:1–13

The Little Man
who Climbed a Tree

Jesus was passing through Jericho. Crowds of
people hurried to meet him. Everyone wanted to see
Jesus.

Zacchaeus wanted to see him too. But he was a
small man. He could not see over the heads of the
crowd. And no one would let him through. People
hated Zacchaeus because he was a cheating tax
collector. He took money from his own people to pay
the Romans. And he kept a large part for himself.

'I'll never be able to see Jesus,' he thought. Then
he had an idea. He ran ahead of the crowd and
climbed a tree. He had a fine view. He could see
Jesus coming. Jesus was right underneath the tree!
Then Zacchaeus nearly fell off his branch in
surprise. Jesus had stopped. He was looking up.

'Climb down quickly, Zacchaeus,' he said. 'I am
coming to stay at your house today.'

Zacchaeus could hardly believe his ears. He
welcomed Jesus to his home with great joy. From
that day on Zacchaeus was a changed man.

'I will give half my money to the poor,' he said.
'And if I have cheated anyone, I will pay him back
four times as much.'

LUKE 19:1–10

The Man who Said Thank You

Jesus came to a village. Outside, standing well away from everyone, were ten men who had leprosy. Because people were afraid of catching it, these men had to leave their homes and friends and live by themselves. Only if the priests said they were well could they ever go home again.

The men called out to Jesus: 'Have pity on us!'

When Jesus saw them, he said: 'Go and let the priests examine you.'

They did as he said, and on the way the signs of their leprosy disappeared and they were well.

One of them came straight back and thanked Jesus for what he had done.

'Didn't I heal ten men?' Jesus said to him. 'Where are the other nine? Are you the only one to give God thanks?'

And he said to the man: 'Stand up, and go on your way. Your faith has made you well.'

LUKE 17:11–19

'Here Comes God's King!'

Jesus was on his way to the capital city – Jerusalem – for the last time. He knew his enemies wanted to kill him, and he warned his disciples that there would be trouble.

People were crowding in from all over the country. Everyone wanted to be there for the great Passover Festival. At Passover time each family ate a special meal, to remind them of how God had rescued the people of Israel from being slaves in Egypt many hundreds of years before.

When they were near Jerusalem, Jesus sent two of his disciples ahead.

'Go to the next village,' he said. 'Untie the donkey you will find there, and bring it here. If anyone asks what you are doing, tell him the donkey is for me.'

The two men did as Jesus told them. They put their cloaks across the donkey's back and helped Jesus to mount.

A great crowd of people were with him. They spread their cloaks on the road in front of Jesus, and waved branches from palm-trees.

'Here comes God's King!' they shouted. 'Praise be to God!'

So Jesus rode into the city, as a king who comes in peace.

MATTHEW 21:1–11

Uproar in the Temple

Next day Jesus went to the Temple. He was very angry. He saw men selling pigeons for people to sacrifice. He saw money-changers giving out the special Temple coins in exchange for Roman ones. They were all cheating the people who had come to the Temple to worship God.

'God's Temple is a place of prayer,' Jesus thundered. 'But you have turned it into a den of thieves!'

He made a whip of rope and drove the animals and people from the Temple, overturning the money-changers' tables.

The place was in an uproar – and the priests were angrier than ever. Jesus must be arrested and put to death.

MATTHEW 21:12–13

The Plot

The religious leaders were jealous of Jesus. The things he said and did made them angry: they thought he was trying to stir people up against them. They were determined to get rid of him.

But they could not think how to do it. For Jesus had many friends among the people.

Then Judas Iscariot, one of the twelve disciples, came secretly to the leaders.

'I will hand Jesus over to you,' he said. 'I can help you to arrest him when no one is about.'

Judas had wanted Jesus to lead a great revolution and free Israel from the Romans. But Jesus would not do it. Angry and disappointed, Judas at last decided to betray Jesus to his enemies.

The leaders were delighted. They agreed to pay Judas thirty silver coins for his part in the arrest.

MATTHEW 26:14–16

Preparing for the Passover

'Where shall we meet for the Passover meal?' the disciples asked Jesus. It was time to get things ready.

'Go into the city,' Jesus said. 'There you will find a man carrying a jar of water. Follow him to his house and tell the owner that I sent you. He will show you a large upstairs room. That is where I want you to prepare the meal.'

The disciples did as Jesus said, and that evening Jesus and the twelve met in the upstairs room. It was their last meal together.

Before they sat down to eat, Jesus took a towel, and poured some water into a basin, and began washing the disciples' feet. Peter hated to see Jesus doing a servant's job, and when it came to his turn he tried to stop him. But Jesus explained that he was showing them something important.

'I have done this as an example,' he said. 'You must never be too proud to serve one another – just as I have served you.'

MARK 14:12–16; JOHN 13:1–17

Never Alone

Jesus knew that he was going to die. He looked so sad, the disciples could see something was wrong. Then he said: 'One of you is going to betray me.'

'Who is it?' whispered John, who was sitting next to Jesus.

'The one to whom I give this bread, dipped in the sauce,' Jesus said. And he gave it to Judas.

'Hurry and do what you have to,' Jesus said to him. So Judas went out into the night.

Jesus talked a lot that night, and the disciples never forgot his words. He spoke to them as his friends. He told them how much he loved them.

'I won't leave you alone,' he said. 'I will come back. And God will give you his Holy Spirit to be with you and help you always. I am going back to God to prepare a place for you.'

While they were eating, Jesus took a loaf of bread, thanked God for it, broke it and shared it amongst them. Then he took a cup of wine, gave thanks to God, and they all drank from it.

Jesus said his death would be like that. They would all share in it. For Jesus was going to be put to death, not for what he had done wrong himself, but for what other people had done.

They sang a last hymn together and the meal was over.

MATTHEW 26:20–30; JOHN 13:21–14:31

62

In the Garden of Gethsemane

After the meal they made their way to the Mount
of Olives. Jesus again warned the disciples of what
was going to happen.

'This very night,' he said, 'you will all run away
and leave me.'

'I never will!' Peter contradicted.

But Jesus said: 'Before cock-crow you will say
three times that you do not know me.'

'Never! I would rather die!' Peter said. And they
all said the same.

When they came to the garden of olive-trees
called Gethsemane Jesus told them to sit down by
the gate and wait while he prayed. But he took
Peter, James and John with him in among the trees.

'Stay with me and keep watch,' he said.

He was very troubled and unhappy.

Then he went a little further on and knelt down

'Father,' he prayed, 'if it is possible, spare me
this suffering. But do what you want, not what I
want.'

Three times he prayed, and three times he went
back to Peter, James and John, and found them
asleep. No matter how hard they tried, they could
not stay awake.

The third time he woke them, they could hear
voices.

'Get up now,' Jesus said. 'They have come to
arrest me.' Now he was ready. His mind was made
up. This was what God wanted him to do.

MATTHEW 26:31–46

65

Betrayed!

People were coming. There were torches at the gate. The guards sent by the religious leaders, led by Judas, had come to arrest Jesus.

'The one I greet with a kiss is the man you want,' Judas explained to the soldiers. Then he went up to Jesus and kissed him. The soldiers closed in.

Jesus did not try to escape or resist arrest. 'Why have you come against me with swords and clubs, as if I were a criminal?' he asked. There was no reply. The soldiers seized him roughly by the arms and marched him off. And all the disciples ran away and left him. But Peter followed at a safe distance.

They took Jesus to the High Priest's house to be questioned by the Sanhedrin Council, the High Court.

After many questions the High Priest asked direct: 'Are you the King, the Son of God?'

'Yes,' Jesus answered, 'I am.'

'You have all heard what the prisoner has said. He claims he is equal to God himself. Do you find him guilty of this crime?'

'Yes, guilty,' shouted the Council. And they demanded that he should be put to death.

But they could not pass sentence without permission from the Roman Governor, Pilate. So early in the morning, they took Jesus to Pilate's headquarters.

MATTHEW 26:47–67

Peter's Ordeal

All this time, Peter was outside in the courtyard.
He joined the guards who were warming
themselves round the fire.

A servant girl walked past, and when she saw
Peter she said: 'You were with Jesus of Nazareth.'

But Peter denied it. He moved away, but she
said to the others: 'This man is one of Jesus'
followers.'

'No. You are wrong. I am not,' said Peter.

Then a little while later, someone else, hearing
him speak, said again: 'You must be one of them. I
can tell by the way you speak that you come from
Galilee too.'

But Peter was now so afraid, he was ready to
swear he had never even met Jesus.

Just then a cock crowed.

Peter remembered how Jesus had said this would
happen. He was very ashamed, and left the
courtyard in tears.

MARK 14:54, 66–72

The Death Sentence

Jesus stood before Pilate.

'He claimed to be a king,' his accusers said. 'And that is treason.'

So Pilate questioned him. But he could find no reason to sentence Jesus to death. He tried to save him, but the crowd would not let him.

'Kill Jesus!' they shouted.

In the end Pilate gave in and sentenced Jesus to death. He was afraid of a riot that would get him into more trouble with the Emperor.

They led Jesus through the city streets to a place called 'The Skull' for execution. They made him carry the heavy wooden cross till he stumbled and fell. Then they ordered one of the crowd of onlookers – a man called Simon – to carry it for him.

At the place of The Skull they nailed him to the cross. A notice above Jesus' head read: 'This is Jesus, the King of the Jews.'

The hot sun beat down, and Jesus was in great pain – but there was no hatred in his heart.

'Forgive them, Father,' Jesus said. 'They don't know what they are doing.'

LUKE 23:13–34

Darkness and Death

Jesus' mother and some of his friends stood near, sharing his pain. Jesus spoke to John:

'Take my mother home,' he said, 'and be a son to her.'

At midday for three hours the land was in darkness. Then Jesus gave a great cry.

'It is finished!' And with these words he died.

The earth shook. And the soldiers on duty at the cross were terrified. 'This man really was the Son of God,' they said.

To make sure that Jesus was dead, one of the soldiers thrust his sword into Jesus' side. Then they took his body down from the cross.

A man called Joseph, who was a follower of Jesus, went to Pilate and asked if he could take Jesus' body away for burial. When Pilate agreed, Joseph and Nicodemus (another of Jesus' friends) took the body and bandaged it with fresh linen.

The women who had followed Jesus from Galilee went with Joseph and saw him put the body of Jesus in a new grave hollowed out of the rock. The men rolled a heavy stone slab across the entrance to close it. Then the women went back home to prepare ointments and spices for anointing the body when the Sabbath rest-day was over.

MATTHEW 27:45–61; JOHN 19:25–42

Jesus is Alive!

After the entrance to the grave had been closed, the chief priests fixed a seal on the stone. And they left guards on watch, to make sure that no one came to steal the body.

But when the women came with their ointments, the grave was open and the body had gone!

Very early on the Sunday morning – Easter Day – there had been an earthquake. God had sent an angel to roll away the stone. The guards were so frightened, they had all run away.

The angel said to the women, 'Don't be afraid. I know you are looking for Jesus. But he is not here. He is alive! Look, this is where his body was. Go quickly and tell the disciples the good news. Tell them they will see him soon.'

In fear and joy the women hurried away. But the disciples would not believe their story. They thought at first that the women had gone out of their minds.

But then some of them came and saw for themselves. The grave was empty. There were the linen bandages which had been wound round the body – lying flat. It was true. Jesus was alive!

MATTHEW 28:1–8; LUKE 24:1–11

Behind Locked Doors

That evening all the disciples were together. The door was locked because they were afraid of the men who had crucified Jesus.

Suddenly Jesus was standing there amongst them.

They were terrified at first. They thought they were seeing a ghost! But Jesus calmed their fears. He showed them the marks of the nails in his hands and feet. Then they knew it was Jesus himself.

'I'm no ghost,' he said, '– feel me and see.'

They were so full of joy at being able to see and talk to Jesus again that they could hardly believe it was true.

Then Jesus said: 'Is there anything to eat?'

They gave him some fish, and watched him eat.

After that there were no more doubts. It was Jesus – and he was real!

Jesus explained how God had planned all that had happened.

'Everything written about me in the Books of Moses, and the prophets, and the Psalms has come true,' he said. 'They foretold how God's promised King would have to suffer and be raised from death on the third day. Now God will forgive all who come to him. This is his Good News for all nations.'

LUKE 24:36–47

'I Shall Always be with You'

Nearly six weeks after Easter Day, the disciples were all together on the Mount of Olives, just outside Jerusalem.

'You are to go out into the whole wide world,' Jesus said, 'and tell people everywhere the Good News. Anyone who believes in me, and is truly sorry for the wrong he has done, will be forgiven. I will give him a new life. Go and make disciples out of every nation, baptizing them and teaching them all that I have taught you. I will help you. I promise, I shall always be with you.'

When he had said this, Jesus was taken up into heaven, to be with God. Two men, dressed in white, spoke to the disciples.

'You have seen Jesus taken up into heaven,' they said. 'One day everyone will see him return.'

They knew then it was no use waiting. They went back to Jerusalem, to begin the work Jesus had given them to do.

MATTHEW 28:19–20; ACTS 1:1–11

Copyright © 1973 Editions Fleurus

Published by
Sandy Lane Books
Sandy Lane West, Oxford, England
ISBN 0 7459 4007 2
Albatross Books Pty Ltd
PO Box 320, Sutherland, NSW 2232, Australia
ISBN 0 7324 1347 8

First published under the title *Evangile pour Toi*
First English language edition © 1976 Lion Publishing
This edition 1995
10 9 8 7 6 5 4 3 2 1 0

Cover picture and illustrations by Noelle Herrenschmidt
French text by René Berthier
English text adapted by Pat Alexander

A catalogue record for this title
is available from the British Library

Printed and bound in Singapore